# FROM GRIEF TO GRACE

# FROM GRIEF TO GRACE

Denisha Karmé

XULON PRESS ELITE

Xulon Press Elite
2301 Lucien Way #415
Maitland, FL 32751
407.339.4217
www.xulonpress.com

Unless otherwise indicated, Scripture quotations taken from the
New King James Version (NKJV). Copyright © 1982 by Thomas
Nelson, Inc. Used by permission. All rights reserved.

Printed in the United States of America.

ISBN-13: 978-1-54566-658-6

This book is for anyone who has
ever felt unworthy of His grace.

# DEDICATION

This book is affectionately dedicated to my sons, Corban and Logan. I pruned and uprooted what seemed to be a generational curse so that you may have a tree, grounded in Christ, with strong, healthy roots. Help me continue cultivating an orchard of grace, love, and kindness. You were made for more. Go live big!

# Acknowledgments

To my hero—my mother! You didn't know it then, but you gave me everything I needed. I watched as you beat yourself up and question your worth. My failures would've been far greater had you not been the one wiping away my tears, talking me through our trials, and just listening to me rattle on . . . when you would rather be relaxing! You gave me the strength to carry on, to look inside myself and see more than failure. You taught me that kindness is everything and courage is powerful. Thank you for all you were to me, which was enough! You are a ruby in my heart!

To my Faith Tabernacle family, thank you for welcoming me into your hearts almost sixteen years ago. I was hurt and confused, yet you gave me room to grow. I admit that it took me longer than it should have to open my own heart, but somehow, I did. Thank you for also loving my children and allowing me to serve as your pastor's wife. You are the family I choose.

To the Georgia District Youth Ministries, thank you for allowing me to share my testimony during a Senior Camp Day Service in 2014. It was the first time that I'd publicly shared my story and, because of that leap of faith, I am at this pivotal spot in my journey. Thank you for believing in me.

To Poppy and Nana, thank you for taking a teenage girl with broken wings under your care. Thank you for mending and nurturing my hurting spirit. You were more than a pastor and pastor's wife to me. I owe so much to you. Thank you for trusting me with a task far greater than I deserved.

Finally, to Michael, you are the dream I never imagined would come true. Your support and encouragement for me to write is a true gift. I am blessed beyond measure to call you mine. I don't deserve you, yet I have you. Sometimes I feel you could have done so much better than me. I know it hasn't been the easiest road with me as your wife but I am grateful for your patience. As long as there is breath in me, I will love you. You give so much to everyone, yet still find the time to make me feel like your queen. I'd spent so much time walking a broken, imperfect path and when the road came to a fork, I looked up and melted into your big brown eyes. I can now see that every trial I ever faced led me straight to you. I will cherish you every day, always. You are now and forever my endless love.

# TABLE OF CONTENTS

# INTRODUCTION

In 2003, I was changed—forever. In an instant, the life of uncertainty that I was all too familiar with . . . *changed*. With no warning or time for preparation, just like that, I had to get used to a new normal. I felt so betrayed by God; I felt as if somewhere, somehow, I had failed. Had I done something wrong? If so, how could I fix it? My life was, by no means, perfect before 2003, but it was consistent and predictable. Little did I know, God was breaking me, hard and fast, for a great work. He couldn't use me where I was or how I was. My breaking cultivated a warrior—but it took years to have the confidence for that warrior to emerge.

This book is my life, my tears, my prayers, my calling. God repaired the holes in my heart and crafted me into an exquisitely hopeful image of grace. I have spent so many days wondering what my brother and my dad would think of my husband or my boys. I find myself getting emotional at Little League baseball games, knowing how proud they would be. I trust that, through God's grace, redemption and restoration were possible before they left this world. I find peace as I feel my brother's encouragement during times of uncertainty. He was my biggest fan and greatest supporter, and through this process, I have found complete healing and purpose for my pain.

As much as it hurts, a loss of people and things is not a loss of purpose. Yes, we stumble, and might possibly lose our way when life throws us a curveball—but we can't lose hope, we can't lose focus, and we can't lose ourselves. God has your back, I can attest for that firsthand. When circumstances come against you, there is no length He won't go to, in order to cover you. Courage comes when you decide to get up. The punches come, I get up. The words cut like the sword of a warrior, I get up. The loss pierces my heart, I get up. Whatever you do, get back up and keep fighting. Do it for yourself because you are worth it.

Remember every raw moment of your journey, from grief to grace. Those moments for me, painful as they were, transformed me into the person I am today. Tether your identity to Christ! When you do so, your identity becomes perfectly predictable and non-reliant on circumstantial things. We lose our sense of stability and control when we leave Christ out of the equation. It becomes easy to make excuses as to why we are not living the life we dream of living. At some point in life we have to be willing to let go of whatever it is that holds us back in order to achieve our goals and dreams.

My identity lies in Christ, not in my past. I don't have to dwell on weekends spent sick, resting on a thrift-store couch because the room was filled with cigarette smoke. Instead, I must believe I was worth more than this world was offering me. Believe in Christ so tenaciously, that even when you feel broken, you can feel His unwavering love sustaining you. I have purposed in my heart to live fully where I desire and how I desire. Doubtful adversaries will always be in your life but they do not have the power to dictate your life.

Don't be afraid to take your journey—start *today*. Stop letting grief take control of your life and allow God's grace to flow into the vulnerable spaces of your heart.

# Chapter 1

## RINGLETS AND RUFFLES
### Twirling with the Winds of Change

"I'm a Queen, crowned in my curls."
— Author Unknown

Never did a Saturday night pass without me having pink sponge rollers in my hair. I was all too proud to look like Shirley Temple at church every Sunday. My ringlets were, by far, my best feature on any given day. My mom could've had her own "Truvy's Salon" with the way she made those ringlets turn out perfectly. Now, girls are using tube socks and all kinds of tricks to prepare their glorious locks to be curled. Sponge rollers were once such a respected addition to any woman's toiletry kit, but now they sit in the dark corner of a cabinet, collecting dust. Oh, the memories I have of sweet conversations with Mama, while she combed out my tangles and rolled my hair.

Moments of happiness, such as a blue dress with the best spinning ruffles you could imagine—those were the memories I chose to hold on to, to make prominent. You see, I never truly appreciated the power of choice or really understood that I was choosing which memories to hold tight. God knew! He knew exactly what I would need in my treasure box of memories to help me through the hard days, the trying days, the days we didn't even expect were coming. My visions of twirling laughter would soon be muddled with tears and a home with only one responsible parent. I didn't even know such a thing existed.

You know, it was almost as if my inner voice was, reminding me to be a little girl and use these moments with my ruffles as a distraction from the chaos unfolding in the background. It was a still small whisper deep down in my spirit saying: Spin around as many times as you can. Enjoy those golden locks bouncing off your cheeks. Layer as many slips—handmade by Nana—as possible under that bold blue dress to add to the fun. Don't look back, focus on the butterflies in your stomach as you twirl . . . not the smell of alcohol in the air or the yelling in the background. Hum once more as you spin your stuffed animals with you . . . and picture a field of daisies all around. Just spin, sweet girl, just keep spinning.

My reality was much different . . . it was full of confusion, rejection, and disappointment. Reality held uncertainty, comparison, and, with it, the feeling that I would never quite measure up.

I am currently parenting a second-grader and, never in a million years, could I picture him able to do the things I did at his age.

Second grade was the first time I can vividly recall memories of feeling inadequate and struggling to process the chaos unfolding in my life . . . second grade! As I mentioned, I have a son in second grade and that brings it full circle for me. It allows me to see how such a fragile piece of God's creation can still flourish, as long as the right people are there to mold and provide guidance. It reminds me to hug, love, and give words of affirmation as often as I can.

I want to begin this chapter by saying that without my mother, I would have never survived the blows dealt to me, especially at such a young age. As long as I could reach her, I felt safe, I felt complete. She made it her mission to overcompensate for the parts missing from my life.

As adorable and happy as the little girl described throughout this chapter may seem, it's nothing more than an illusion. Much like the highlight reels on Instagram, Facebook, and lifestyle blogs, my childhood pictures of glee were my vintage 90s (as my children call it) highlight reel. Fairy tales are the dreams of every little girl; they are the reality we all believe our life will truly transform into. Oh, but how life can be a cruel, hard teacher. I learned a long time ago that with a little faith, kindness, and courage, fairy tales can most certainly become a reality. We can all experience a fairy tale if we are willing to endure the hardship that is attached to real life. It's all about your reactions and what you choose to do with whatever circumstances life has given you. Believe you can have more—then go out and find it!

Life, just like the fancy twirling dresses, has layers and we sometimes have to dig through and stay in one layer a little longer than we might desire. That's okay, sweet girl, you aren't alone. Just fluff the lace and power through the itching, it won't always be this way. Sometimes you just have to scratch your way to the surface.

What little girl doesn't love ruffles? Just like each person's innate differences, ruffles come in all shapes and sizes, as well as most every demographic of life.

Ruffles hug every little girl no matter where she comes from. The hugs can be rough and scratchy, but you can always count on them!

I've seen ruffles in the mud, ruffles with heels, ruffles with high-top Converses, ruffles with a soccer ball, ruffles with a baby doll, ruffles gracing crossed ankles, ruffles that have been ripped from chasing boys, ruffles caressing wildflowers, ruffles causing tears from their incessant itching . . . and my favorite, ruffles twirling in the wind!

Whatever memory you have of ruffles, I'm positive it's a good one and, if not, I know it puts a smile on your face. Maybe you loved your Sunday debut in ruffles or maybe you fought your mom tooth and nail about wearing them. Ruffles were, no doubt, a part of your weekly childhood routine.

I lived in a constant state of imaginary Cinderella as I was tossed and turned by life's hurricanes, one after another. Fairy tales were a welcome distraction from the noise and clouds of cigarette smoke. A castle with Prince Charming, riding to rescue you from your otherwise tumultuous life, may be far-fetched, but to a child it may be a reprieve. Eventually, fairy tales turn into unrealistic, distant dreams as you mature and grow.

Those child-like moments of faith are the very ones that we sometimes look back on as we say a small prayer of renewed spiritual energy. I am positively confident that we create our reality. Life may show us the havoc that it can wreak, but we can choose how it shapes us. We will talk more about that later.

Second grade was my first year, ever, to step foot in a public school. Prior to that, my grandmother paid for us to attend a private Christian school. My mom worked five to six days a week and so we had to make financial cuts in several areas.

Of course, as a child, I didn't understand the financial side of it, so I can honestly say, I never felt like I didn't have enough. I never understood that tomato soup and grilled cheese was a "cheap meal." In fact, I still crave this dynamic duo and keep it in stocked in my pantry. No matter the type of day my mother had, there was always a home-cooked meal on our table.

Now, as a parent looking back, there seems to be a missing component of parenting in the twenty-first century—togetherness inside the home. We hurry through the fast food drive-through and on to the next thing on our schedule. When we give our children our time, and truly engage with them, it means so much more than handing them a twenty-dollar bill at Target.

I encourage you to stop, slow down, and take a moment to have good conversation with your family around the dinner table. I never felt like I'd missed out on the latest, greatest fads because my mom made up for it with love. My home was disrupted on almost every front, but sitting around the dinner table and having meaningful conversations was one thing we had going for us. Maybe it's because we are Southern or maybe it's because we needed just one thing that could be consistent in our home. Whatever the reason for my Mom doing this, I am thankful!

My brother was in the fourth grade, two years ahead of me and already had some learning trouble. So, our particular educational change in my opinion, as an adult looking back, was a good one. We were surrounded by educators who truly were invested in helping my mom and being a part of her support team. This was vital, considering the tsunami that was soon to hit our lives.

My brother and I came in the house one afternoon to find my dad sitting on the couch with my mom. I will never forget the way his hands moved as he said, "I am leaving today. Your mom and I are changing. I am going one way and she is moving another." That sentence still echoes in my mind like a horror movie. I knew my life was being torn apart and changing, but my tiny mind just couldn't anticipate how much.

My days were focused on spinning in my ruffles and being distracted by my imagination. All I wanted to do was play—instead of being forced to grow up immediately and take on the kind of responsibility that no child should have to face.

As my father sat speaking to us, he held his hands the way a doctor does when he is making sure you don't have a concussion after a bad fall . . . his index fingers were pointed up and pressed against each other while the rest of his hands made fists. Then he pulled them apart as he attempted to illustrate how he and my mother were traveling on different paths. His fingers moved apart in the same way that he was ripping our family apart. I remember the confused feeling in my head and my heart.

I didn't quite know how to express my concerns and, if I would have, did he even care to listen? Did I get a vote? Why was this happening?

From that moment forward, there were few happy moments with my father present. No amount of excuses and no matter how many times I was told, "He loves you with all his heart," made the choice he was making all right. It didn't make any of it right. It didn't make me happy and, worst of all, being told he loved me didn't help me to forgive him.

I grew up listening to everyone make excuses for him—why he chose the road he did, and frankly, I didn't care why. I cared that he'd walked away from me instead of fighting to be in my life, like I knew he could fight. After all, he was a soldier and had gone overseas before I was born. How was this less important? How could he choose to allow an addiction to win this battle? I just wanted him to want our family and look further down the road to the struggles he was setting in place in our lives.

My father left me with a void. For years, I felt it was my fault. Thank God for husbands! My husband was my perfect gift, teaching me the value and role of a father. I know . . . I am a Christian woman of God and how in the world could I have these feelings? But I wasn't always the woman I am today. I needed more than mere words. I needed to feel, to know they were true.

I spent my childhood visiting my dad every other weekend, at whichever government apartment he was in at the time. Other times, I visited him in a jailhouse with a thick glass partition separating us. We talked through a black phone and sat on a cold metal stool. My mom would make the best of it by taking us to Taco Bell or McDonald's, or we might play baseball in the front yard or go on a walk through our neighborhood. But mostly she helped by just being there.

As I sat and wrote these pages, I cried so hard that I couldn't catch my breath. I do realize just how blessed I am to have had my mom and found my husband. But I've found that my wounds haven't completely healed and my eyes have been opened to just how deep my hurt runs. I had never valued forgiveness and the sweet gift it is and was to me before now! As far back as I can see, God's grace has been present in my life.

My mom would sing while she was vacuuming and, even though at the time I was consumed in my conversations with my stuffed animals, I can still close my eyes and hear the sweet sound of her singing in the background:

*"He's been faithful, faithful to me.*
*Looking back, His love and mercy I see.*
*Though in my heart I have questioned and I've failed to believe, yet*
*He's been faithful, faithful to me."*

I know that only her faith in God and her drive to survive kept us together. It was she who allowed me to hope for more. Early on, I felt a desire to have something better than just a temporary fix to get me through my daily grind. My mother worked tirelessly to make sure that I had a way out, that I would always have choices about how to live, or even whether to live at all. I had exclusive rights to my story and there wasn't a person in my life I would let would write it for me.

Anyone who knows me, well knows that I am strong-willed and stubborn. My mom used to say I was hard-headed . . . my kids say I'm a "sassy, Southern mama." I do honestly try to keep my flesh in line! However, I can also be dependent in the way that I don't want to be alone. This can be unhealthy if you surround yourself with the wrong people and believe the lies that they tell you about yourself, or worse, become what they say you are when you know or feel that it is not right.

There was a line fed to me once by someone whom I truly admired and believed wanted me to succeed. I believed he was in my corner, rooting for me! I remember being so excited to meet with him, thinking he would encourage me, tell me that, despite the odds, I was growing into the little lady God wanted me to be. Boy, was I wrong!

He said, "You have your father's DNA and that means addiction is in your blood. One taste of alcohol, cigarettes, or drugs will have you hooked. Because of this, you will live in a constant struggle and be tempted at every turn. Those chains already bind you."

His words echoed in my mind as I realized this meeting wasn't a reassuring, "You are doing a great job" one. He was literally validating all my hidden fears about myself. He was confirming that my identity revolved around the choices my father had made. There was no positive reinforcement happening. I was being emotionally defaced and, the unfortunate truth was, I'm not sure he was aware of the colossal misdirection of the conversation. My heart ached with the realization that, no matter how hard I tried to create my own path or escape from the shadows of an addiction that wasn't my own, it would always be a hindrance to my involvement in church. This was only one time in a series of me being made an outcast or being the one who was destined to fail because "she came from a dysfunctional family."

I became immune to the looks of disapproval and allowed them to completely consume my thoughts. I allowed the opinion of others dictate the way I saw myself. I am ashamed of the things my stubbornness drove me to, just to prove I had a different destiny. Immaturity and a lack of positive counsel had me traveling down a road that I had, long ago, promised myself I wouldn't repeat. I assumed my worth based off of someone else's ignorance. These are struggles that can haunt me even as an adult.

So, there I was, stuck in a state of insecurity and self-doubt, wondering if I would ever measure up. Would I ever be enough? Who could possibly want this damaged, problematic girl?

Hurt is a peculiar thing and it can crush us or it can strengthen us. I fought long and hard to be in the place I am today and, without a doubt, it was worth every second of effort to get here. I learned a lot about myself during my teenage years.

Yes, I had a mouth the size of Texas and probably embarrassed my mom more times than I care to admit, but I also learned that I was a fighter! I was a warrior! I was brave! I was a child of the King and there wasn't one person who could take that from me. I was not that person some tried to say I was. No, I was the girl whom God created and chose to be part of a bigger plan!

I was stronger than my circumstances.

The enemy expected me to believe the lie that I didn't matter enough for anyone to be able to see past my flaws, past my bloodline, past the scars that rejection had left on my life. Do you know what? I did believe that lie. I accepted the false fact that I would be stuck in the cycle of addiction that was my family tree. I would never be enough for any man.

Or so I thought . . .

You see, once upon a time, I was a little petite girl with blonde ringlets twirling my troubles away in a blue ruffled dress!

*Chapter 2*

# MISUNDERSTOOD

## Divorce and Fitting In

"Hardships often prepare ordinary people
for an extraordinary destiny."
— C. S. Lewis

Girls can be so vindictively mean. Most times we are a product of our environment and, as children, we only behave the way adults in our circle do. Nonetheless . . . girls can be so mean!

I learned way too early what it means to be unfairly judged. I learned just how ugly our carnal, fleshly nature could be. I learned that there were no better friends than Jesus, my stuffed animals, and my mom. It felt like a constant reality show audition, just trying to find my place among my peers. So much of my childhood was spent relying on my brother because he was a friend who understood me.

Our parents divorced when I was very young. My dad stopped going to church and soon became homeless, all because of addiction. My mom worked sixty-hour weeks and most Saturdays—all so we could survive. I wish I'd known then what I know now, because it would have been easier to walk away from hurtful people. Ignorance can cause people, especially young and immature people, to behave in an ugly manner and say hurtful things.

If I could look back and tell my younger self anything, it would be simple:

*Keep your spirit soaring high and never miss an opportunity to show kindness.*

So many times, I fought fire with fire because that's what I assumed made you strong. On top of that, I felt like I had nothing to lose.

I mean . . . this was my life, nothing was going to change. People are people and I would be misinterpreted for the rest of my days! I was too young to comprehend the power to change my perspective and my outcome was in my hands, not someone else's.

This too shall pass. . . .

Why do people say that? Do I believe it? Why me? Did I do something wrong? Am I just not good enough? Will I ever be important?

These were questions that I remember contemplating during those lonely years of feeling different from all the girls in my youth group. Nights spent crying to my mom who, at the time, was my only friend about the "mean girls." There was one thing that still sticks out in my mind and that is her saying, "Kill them with kindness."

I mean, after all, she was my mother and it was her job to say that I was pretty, smart, talented, and good enough. How was she able to encompass so much wisdom, love, and kindness toward people? Even those people who always seemed to have disappointed her. She ultimately saw good in everyone. God built this woman to be my mom and there is no doubt about that!

The problem in all this was that I never believed it was true. Even now, as a thirty-two-year-old grown woman, I struggle with self-doubt. The inadequacies I believed about myself were deep-seated. I chose as a young lady to believe the worst in myself, because it seemed to be where I was destined to travel. Thank goodness, I serve a God who knows better than I.

My negative self-talk grew to such an out-of-control level. . .. I'm still working on it, but I can confidently say that I love myself now and, previously, I'd never been able to. The first time I ever watched the new *Cinderella* movie, I cried, as I'm sure you did as well! I could literally relate to her when her mother said, "Ella, have courage and be kind."

It was like I was flashing back to moments at home with my mom. For instance, the conversations she had with me . . . while we were in the car waiting for my brother to finish a baseball practice and eating our chicken-and-rice casserole dinner out of Tupperware containers. She always reminded me that we can't repay hurt with hurt. Simply ignore it and keep going. It doesn't matter what they think . . . they will fall from their high horse one day. Those were all the life lessons I had to keep on repeating, when I really just wanted to give them a piece of my mind.

I was nowhere close to being Cinderella! She was good and beautiful. We lived in a separate universe. She was a person of unequivocal beauty, brains, kindness, energy, and she got the guy!

See? I told you I'm still working on my negative self-talk and gaining confidence.

Do you ever stop and wonder how she got all that cleaning and cooking done every day? It is absolutely mind-boggling! This is a perfect example of comparison and why women shouldn't watch TV. At all. *Ever.*

My story of loss and motherly advice is relatable to hers and YES, I most certainly got the guy of my dreams, too! My own modern-day Prince Charming. I have learned through my awkward teenage years that beauty is more inward than outward. Did your mom ever tell you, "It's what's on the inside that counts"? I'm sure you are flashing back right now, picturing yourself scowling at your mom or dad as she or he smiled with pride! It's so true, we must be as diligent in working on our inner beauty as our outer.

*"Have courage and be kind."*

Courage is the strength to keep going even when the situation gets really difficult. You must persevere and embrace the mind-set that you are worth more than failure. You are worth more than what your peers have been brainwashing you into believing. They may say that you are inconsequential, inferior, or a loser. Whatever they say, have the strength to push through the bad days and know that a certain set of circumstances will not define your future unless you allow them to. Who is they anyways? Whoever they are, they have no idea who you are and what you are capable of. You are in control of your destiny, not they.

I want to show you your inner and outer beauty. You are uniquely you, a person God designed you to be. It doesn't matter what the girl next to you is doing or what her size is. Be healthy— both physically and mentally!

> Psalm 27:14, NKJV: "Wait on the Lord; Be of good courage, and he shall strengthen your heart; Wait, I say on the Lord."

Do me a favor: take a moment and get lost in your thoughts. I want you to believe you deserve more because . . . guess what? You do!

Deep down inside each one of us lies a warrior, awaiting our approval to rise to the occasion. If you struggle with insecurities and negative self-comparison, spend the next thirty days in gratitude. You aren't allowed to say one negative thing about yourself! The Bible is stuffed full of men and women who were courageous against all odds. You are no exception!

Kindness is grace in action. People do not have to deserve it in order for us to give it. Just like Christ freely gives us His grace when we are so often underserving, we can afford the same graciousness to those who hurt us. Kindness is a smile that speaks volumes when words can't. My mother knew then what I know now and that is: kindness has power!

It's the type of power that frightens those holding their status over our head. Some refer to kindness as *weakness*, but it wins every single time. It takes hard work, because you have to constantly look at your reflection and snap it into submission. That untamed, unhinged carnal side that we all hide deep down wants to emerge from the cold, dark shadows and scream: "Here I am! You want a piece of me?"

So, girls, in my experience as an awkward little lady, I found that people are people and people can be mean! In school, I was always the last to finish laps around the track because I had zero endurance. I even attempted to fake asthma to get out of running a mile (yes, I know—not my finest moment).

I did half as many sit-ups. Every. Single. Time. Don't even ask about my experiences with basketball. Complete and utter failure comes to mind. The few things I did with excellence, no one ever knew about, because I was typically too shy to put myself out there. I was a bit of a loner and, because of that, I harshly judged myself. I could never quite put my finger on how I could make myself be like the other girls in my youth group at church. It was because I was different. I wasn't supposed to be like the other girls. I was supposed to be me and with confidence. Most of my days were spent feeling misunderstood and that caused rejection and anger to take root in my spirit.

Now, as a pastor's wife, I encourage the girls and women to express their differences. I absolutely love taking a look around our congregation and seeing different styles and stages of life. No matter the differences, we are all friends who have turned into family. We spend too much time trying to be like the girl next to us, when God just wants us to be the girl He created! We can never fully understand why God conditions us in life the way He does, but I do see that my molding on the potter's wheel was purposeful!

> 2 Corinthians 12:9 (NKJV) says: "And He said to me, 'My grace is sufficient for you, for My strength is made perfect in weakness.' Therefore, most gladly I will rather boast in my infirmities, that the power of Christ may rest upon me."

Michelle Graham wrote it like this: Shame says that because I am flawed, I am unacceptable, Grace says that though I am flawed, I am cherished.

I love that word, *cherished*. It means to hold or treat as dear, or to care for tenderly. Wow! That is so special, to know that even though my earthly father was incapable of cherishing me and though I was misunderstood by my peers, I have a heavenly Father who will cherish me and who will always be there for me. I am made whole in Him and He is that strength I need when I feel weak and alone.

We were created to stand out, not fit in, so why do we spend so much time fighting that? Most of our days are spent trying to tailor ourselves and be like the girl on the other side of the room—all because her Instagram is perfect. That doesn't mean her life is! Social media has given us an all-access pass to the highlight reel of complete strangers' lives and, because of that, we find it difficult to view them as anything other than perfect robots.

Let me tell you something: that girl across the room doesn't live pain-free. She has flaws, she's far from perfect, and she, just like you, has been fearfully and wonderfully made! I know we hear that often as girls, but it still remains one of my favorite scriptures.

> Psalm 139:14, NKJV: "I will praise You, for I am fearfully and wonderfully made; marvelous are Your works, and that my soul knows very well."

You see, it's quite logical—God doesn't make mistakes. His work is marvelous, and you, my dear girl, are a work whom He created. There is no question of your worth.

**A lesson I had to learn:** I can't control people! I can, however, love them and sometimes, that can change their outlook.

We are all entitled to our own opinions and, sure, you can even share them out loud if you want. Ultimately, you have to decide who you want to be and what you want to get out of life, but also . . . what do you want to offer? If sharing your opinion only gets the words off your chest or unproductively does more harm than good, then you have to ask yourself, "Is it worth it?" Take a long look at the person causing you grief.

Maybe she behaves in a "competitive/I'm better than you" way because of her own insecurities! Stop! Take a moment to really think about that. We are not only comparing ourselves to someone else—but we are changing *who we are* based off who we think someone else is. We change our style, our convictions, our diets and anything else trending at the time all based on someone's social media post of the day. That is not their whole story. What you see on the internet is like a half truth, it's what you comprehend their life to be but most likely not complete reality. Be the person that you want to be. What makes you happy? Think about that girl you are envious of; her life could very well be falling apart at the seams. It could be worse than your situation. Have you ever stopped to think that maybe the person who drives you bonkers is treating you and everyone else with disdain because of their own unhappiness?

**Think About This:**

**Maybe**: I can control my reaction to her behavior.

**Maybe**: I can smile and look past what I now can see is ignorance. And hey, ignorance is not bliss, in my opinion. I firmly believe that knowledge is power!

**Maybe**: That person who really cooks your grits is threatened by the idea of being made irrelevant or obsolete. She could be on a mission to prove she can be more and you're over here getting offended that she might be judging you.

Stop worrying about everyone else! No matter the reason, "her" behavior will not control what you do or how you feel about yourself. In a sense, you gain compassion when you shift your perspective. So, I am going to encourage you to do what I, myself, am learning to do. <u>Shift your focus!</u>

Shift your focus from how you *feel* to what you *know*. You can be mistaken by what you think you see. Look through the eyes of knowledge and courage and confidently follow God's plan for your life, regardless of what everyone around you thinks. Don't be afraid to be you! I wish I had someone other than my mom telling me that I was meant for greater things. Quit surrendering your life to labels given to you by ignorant opinions. The pen isn't in just anyone's hand, it's in the hands of Jesus Christ and only He can author your story. Don't let anyone else's inability to let go of the past control your right now or the future you are designed to have.

I understand the way things used to be, but times are changing. Be careful when you decide to judge a friend's circumstances, based on your own. Your only job in her life is to be there for her, talk to her, and reassure her that she is not dirty just because life tossed her a rotten lemon.

Free yourself from the burden of being perfect. Find joy in the middle of the chaos because, unfortunately, divorce is messy and fitting in is overrated!

*Chapter 3*

# THE FIGHT OF MY LIFE
## Grief and Loss

"When it rains, looks for rainbows, when it's dark, look for stars."
— Oscar Wilde

M y senior year of high school started out with transition and change, only it wasn't the kind I'd been planning for since freshman year. I had just moved to a new church, on my own— without my mom, but with her blessing. I was excited about all the new opportunities, friendships, and involvement that a church in the United Pentecostal Church International (UPCI) organization could offer. My life, leading up to this point, had allowed me to gain what some would consider an unhealthy amount of independence. I knew my own mind and was all too skilled at speaking it! This moment was climactic and had been brewing inside of me for what seemed like forever. I wanted happiness, normality, and freedom from the bondage that shadowed my life. I wanted to be in a place where no one knew my past failures influenced by a father who'd shamed my house. I wanted conversations that didn't start or end with legal terms. No more talks that left me feeling as if I was the one tattered and torn by addiction. I wanted to be free to be me!

Little did I know, this year would transform my life in such a way that, fifteen years later, I would be composing a book about it. The series of events that I viewed as failures were literally catapulting me into ministry. Not just any ministry, but one that could and most certainly *would* empower men, women, boys, and girls to go and become the wonderful person that God designed them to be.

There was no way to know that the countless hours of sitting through *Rocky* movie marathons with my brother were about to pay off. *Rocky* taught me one thing: when life gets you down, you have the choice to get up and fight, or let it defeat you. It may take everything you have, but it is worth it to make a difference and feel God's purpose at work in your life!

> *"One step at a time. One punch at a time. One round at a time."* — *Rocky Balboa*

A month or so into this transition, I was having dinner with some of the church youth. It was just a normal night for me. I got home around 9:00 p.m. to hear the phone ringing. When I answered, a man told us that my brother had been arrested and there was a problem while transporting him. They had taken him to the local hospital and we needed to come as soon as possible.

We drove for what seemed like hours! I remember walking into a cold building, numb and completely unprepared for what was coming. Unfortunately, this was something I had grown accustomed to; it was nothing unusual for my mom to receive a phone call like this about my brother. He lived at home with us, and was out of jail at the time, but he had been gone for weeks—with no call or no indication of where he was.

Everything was moving at high speed and I was stuck in time! I walked to a closed room and looked through the window while my mom stood talking to the doctor. I saw my brother lying on a table with those medical paddles shocking his body. My heart was in my stomach. I knew my life was about to change forever.

I had never seen anything like this before. His clothes were all over the floor, and there were wires and machines cluttering up the small room.

*What are they doing? Why didn't anyone help him before it was too late? Why is that nurse drinking a Mountain Dew and laughing?*

A million questions rushed through my head . . . almost as if I were having a dream that was quickly turning into a nightmare! I couldn't move; I was stuck inside my body, screaming for answers, but no one was listening to me! I just wanted to wake up, safe in my bed, and walk across the hall to see my brother sleeping. *This is all just a dream and I'll wake up soon*, I told myself.

We watched as the staff hung their heads in disappointment after working to save him for as long as they could. We sat in an empty room. Doctors and police officers explained an intense story of unfortunate events that had resulted in a mother losing a son. I was so confused, numb, and angry. I was cold, shaking, and lonely.

Just a simple traffic stop? Not quite!

My brother was on probation and in possession of drugs . . . crystal meth, actually, which was a quick ticket to jail. In an effort to hide the drugs, he'd put the bag in his mouth, which dissolved, and the rest was history. He acted fearless when it came to experimenting with drugs, but this time was different. He didn't intend to die. He didn't mean to kill himself. He was a boy, trying to work the system so it wouldn't work against him. This time he lost, we lost, and it wasn't a game.

There were no take-backs. This choice that he, no doubt, intended to brag about later, instead took his ability to speak at all. His heart was so big and compassionate. If only he could have seen in himself the potential that I saw. Maybe I could have done more.

I stood by the bed where he lay, charcoal still smeared on his face from their unsuccessful efforts to pump all the drugs out of his body. Still unable to show emotion, I silently begged God to change this outcome. The doctors had first called my mom by herself. They told her it was time to say "goodbye." There was nothing more they could do.

She moved over to me and the words that came out of her mouth were like fire to my flesh. I didn't want to hear them. "I know you don't want to, but you have to go. You need to say goodbye and tell him you love him. You will regret it if you don't."

I walked in the room with my mom by my side. I touched his hand, still warm, and there, in that brief second, was when I woke up from my dreamlike state. Reality slapped me in the face. It was a nightmare of grief that I had no idea how to survive.

I pleaded with God. "Please, he is my protector! He is my best friend! I cannot do life without him!"

Why did every bad decision hurt so much? This decision wasn't even my own! Someone else was molding my future and . . . why? I didn't understand any of it and I didn't welcome it.

There was nothing I could do. This storm was out of my control and I had no answers. But I did have a million questions.

*This is too much! I can't do this! I'm not strong enough. I won't survive this storm! I am literally in the eye of a hurricane with no lifeboat in sight!*

You know, in all my wondering and frustrated confusion, I still held on to God. I was all too familiar with loneliness and rejection, and my brother was the one person I could always count on. That dark, bitter, and empty Friday night altered my life in a way I could have never prepared for. I was alone in a world I didn't understand.

Soon after the loss of my brother, pain settled in and became a constant companion of emotion at the core of my very being. I was barely existing. Happiness was unattainable, or so I thought. I honestly felt like I didn't deserve any better.

My life had been a continual series of storms.

I stopped going to school, the way I should, and spent every day going to the cemetery.

*Alone . . . is this what you have for me, God? If so, I don't accept it! I just can't! Remember, I'm stubborn, God. You created me, but I don't want the ache and pain that comes with being alone. What am I supposed to do now? One thing my dad taught me was how to throw a punch, so I will fight. I'm going to fight my way back down this broken path, back to life.*

The last thing I wanted to hear were the well-meaning conversation starters that felt like a way of making it less awkward for the other person. "I'm sorry!" or "He's in a better place." I didn't want him in a better place. His best place was with me! My dad somehow managed to pull himself out of his addiction to come to the funeral home and that was the first time I had seen him in many, many years. I can still picture him, staring at me and saying, "You're not a little girl anymore. I never get to see you."

*Seriously? What did you expect? You walked away, remember?*

He'd missed everything in our lives and, honestly, I was angry that he had the nerve to stand there and speak to me as if it were my fault that he'd missed my growing-up years.

As I'm sure you can piece together at this point, my spirit was in trouble . . . bitterness had crept in and I was one angry young woman! Inside, I was screaming:

*Why did you do this to our family? How could you leave us to this fate?* I was barely standing, much less surviving this storm.

Once the service was over and all the meals were delivered, the dust seemed to settle. People called less and stopped dropping by. My mom went back to work and it was then that my grief showed its ugly face. Feelings would start rushing over my body, and I wasn't exactly prepared for the pain that accompanied those raw emotions.

I distinctly remember sitting in a cold, empty cemetery on a cloudy day, completely broken. I was no stranger to the agonizing sting of rejection, but this unbearable loss—how would I come back? How would I recover? The clouds hovered over me as if to tell me, "There is no hope. You are a lost cause. The conclusion of your story will not differ from this. Why even try?"

The once colorful flowers on my brother's grave had begun to wither, much like my soul. There was a chill in the air, which seemed to follow me everywhere. Loneliness was very present in my life. I began to cry, on this specific day, hot tears flowing down my face as I prayed for my pain to end. I remember asking God, "Isn't there a river where I can drink and never thirst again? Will it consume my pain and fill my heart with peace? How can I tap into your presence, God? I need you, now!"

I wish I could say it didn't take many mistakes to finally make my way back to happiness, but, in fact, I did turn to several wrong things before turning to God and deciding I wanted my life to make a difference. I finally came to a place where I could talk to my mom. That day I left the cemetery and went to her job. I sat in a metal chair at her work, begging her to help me.

She made one simple statement:

"You can be happy! You are still alive and you cannot allow this pain to control your life."

How could she give me such sound advice when she must have been dying on the inside? Guilt completely riddled my being anytime a hint of a smile snuck across my face. The blame game was so intense in our small circle and I knew my mother, as perfect as she was to me, was tearing herself apart . . . yet she loved me enough to pull me out of such a dark pit. My world was and is always better because of her! I knew in that moment that I could and would survive my grief. I didn't quite know how and I suppose that was okay, but in fact, I would survive.

I truly had no earthly idea how I could be happy and not let this grief control my life, but I was not willing to let my unhappiness take another child from my mother. I had to try, if not for me, then for her. So, I fought! I put on my boxing gloves and threw myself into serving at my church and telling everyone: "I'm good. God is good. Life is good."

My "good" was a Band-Aid covering a small scrape that was getting smaller and smaller on the outside, but internally (you know the place where no one else can see) I was close to defeat. My heart, my mind, my soul, those things were like a teapot, ready to explode! I somehow managed to graduate high school, move out on my own, and find a really good job after putting myself through orthodontic assisting school. Still, I was fighting to be more than I was born to be, but never dealing with the terminal hurt inside. One day at a time, I was determined to have a good life, but without realizing it, I was punishing myself for surviving by allowing negativity and discontent to set up permanent residence in my spirit.

Almost two years after my brother's accidental overdose, I received a phone call from one of my dad's friends—one who usually called us when my dad needed some money or help of some kind. She said Dad had been robbed and murdered. I couldn't trust her information and there was a moment where I almost ignored it, because I was so accustomed to drunk or high phone calls from my father and his random friends. He passed my contact information around like it was free bubble gum.

After sitting, waiting, and dwelling, I decided to check on her story. So, I went through several channels of police departments. That path eventually had me on my way to the GBI, the Georgia Bureau of Investigation.

The police had found a body earlier that day and his finger prints were a match with my fathers. Since my parents were divorced and I was the next of kin, I had to go identify the body, in case it really was my dad. The dead man had been beaten, but thankfully, the first blow had killed him, so there was no suffering. The 30 minute drive from Covington to Atlanta seemed to take hours. The car ride was quiet. Pretty soon, I started shivering in panic as memories came rushing back from the night my brother died.

My mom was on vacation when I received the news of my father's death and so I wouldn't be alone, my then boyfriend drove me to the Police Station and never left my side through that dreadful process. I remember the touch of his hand on my lap and how I felt so unworthy of his love. Inadequacy flooded my mind, along with thoughts of self-doubt, self-destruction, and self-sabotage. He had to think I came with too much baggage, as his family was so well put together. This was the second time he'd accompanied me through the grief of losing a loved one. I was so ashamed of my life!

I will never forget what it felt like to be questioned in an interrogation room and how they left me to wait in an empty, cold room with a disgusting cup of coffee. The authorities had to determine that they were correctly identifying the dead man. After a long period of silence, the detective confirmed that it was, indeed, my father.

I felt so lost and alone! My mom was out of town. I was only nineteen. How I longed for my blue ruffled dress, simpler days, and those distant memories of laughter with my family!

In my mind, I went completely numb and wondered, why had this happened? I can't go through this again! Even through my pain, I was determined to come through this just like before, with my brother. But the truth was, I hadn't really come through before. My emotional train was about to derail in a severe way, but I was buckled in for the ride and couldn't get off this fast-moving atrocity! My anger was growing more dangerous by the second. I found that losing my dad brought about a different type of grief. I'd lost his presence in my life at such a young age that I had almost already grieved his loss, but now I was just angry at what he'd done to me, what he'd left me to deal with. There I was, left picking up the broken pieces of our lives and trying to make sense of it all.

**Addiction and Breaking:**

Addiction is a selfish disease! Dictionary.com says addiction is the state of being enslaved to a habit or practice or to something that is psychologically or physically habit forming, such as narcotics, to such an extent that its cessation causes severe trauma.

Wikipedia says addiction is a brain disorder, characterized by compulsive engagement in rewarding stimuli, despite adverse consequences.

You see, putting these substances into our bodies, whether they be drugs, alcohol, opioids, nicotine, etc., eventually creates a dependency where your body literally cannot function without them. This is called withdrawal and, when you get to that point, if you aren't properly monitored, you can harm either yourself or someone you care about.

Life has taught me these things, not through a book or a fancy degree, but from living amid the horror of someone else's addiction. Waiting in the shadows to see how this bender would play out, how the latest obsession would affect me. So many days I spent alone, wondering what I had done wrong. I often felt second best or unworthy of experiencing happiness.

Yet again, instead of dealing with my grief, I threw myself into church and work. About six months had passed, I was now engaged and my fiancé was serving as the youth pastor at our church. I kept myself plenty busy between helping him, working, and planning a wedding. I thought I was doing a great job of hiding my pain and ignoring my need for closure. To be honest I was angry, sad, and lonely all at the same time but I was clueless as to why because I never really allowed myself to deal with my feelings.

Then came a Friday night youth service. It should have been just like any other Friday night, but the load of grief I'd been carrying inside reached a point of maximum capacity. The amount of stress I could absorb had been overloaded for so long. This all culminated in a grand collapsing moment. Outwardly, I had quietly powered through every stage of grief. Inwardly, I'd been corroding away. However, I always made sure to keep the visible parts of my life seem like I was doing great.

Suddenly, there I was, literally in a fetal position in the floor of my husband's office—crying harder than I ever had before. The poor guy had no idea what to do for me. My heart was aching and I didn't know how to express my pain.

So, after admitting defeat and acknowledging that I didn't know how to help myself, I started grief counseling. This decision was a life-changing one for me. That time in my life cultivated me into a warrior! I dug to the deepest depths of my soul and found the courage to live!

Courage is a peculiar thing. It appears to lie dormant inside our spirit until we activate its power, which allows us to journey to higher mountains. We put on our armor, pick up our sword, and take care of business.

> Psalm 56:3, NKJV: "When I am afraid I will put
> my trust in you."

I was sitting in my mother-in-law's living room and, as we were watching the Thanksgiving Day parade, a song from *Cinderella* came on:

*"A dream is a wish your heart makes, when you're fast asleep.*
*In dreams, your will lose your heartaches.*
*Whatever you wish for, you keep.*

*Have faith in your dreams and someday your rainbow will come
smiling through.
No matter how your heart is grieving, if you keep on believing, the
dream that you wish will come true."*

It's funny, as an adult woman, how I can get the same butterflies
I did as a little girl. I sat listening to the lyrics of this decades-old
Disney classic, and the happiness and family environment surrounding me seemed to freeze in time. I started choking back tears
and thinking how these words applied to my life . . . and how, long
ago, I had made a wish that was coming true—not just because of
my faith, but because of prayers.

A dream is my favorite thing—that is, if it takes away your heartache. I can have faith in God's process or waiting, but just how long
must I wait for my rainbow? This was the moment I found my
strength. How could a Disney song be the *light bulb moment* my
mind needed?

Regardless of how silly it may seem, there it was—my moment
of truth. Those nights upon nights, spent wondering if I would ever
see a rainbow? They were gone, and I vowed to do something I
was unfamiliar with and honestly didn't know how to do. . . . I was
going to trust.

Wow! Just saying it aloud took a lot out of me. I could do it.
After all, Jesus got on the cross for me, so I can trust Him with my
future healing and happiness. I'd spent so long standing on the ledge.
My life had been a series of hurricanes and I was currently living
through the most devastating one yet. So, there I was, stepping out

into this hurricane with nothing but a tote bag full of wishes and faith. You have to be a warrior to have the bravery to step out and go *all in*, but why not try? After all, I had nothing left to lose.

*How long must I endure the shaping and molding of my spirit?*, I asked. *How long should I remain on the potter's wheel before you are done, God? I don't know if I can take any more and I have no idea what you are preparing me for.* Most of my fight was spent arguing with God and, quite frankly, I was about ready to fall off the cliff's ledge, angry with God. Then, I chose to give every trial, every heartache, every doubt, and every insecurity to Him. Then came the sunshine!

I was in the fight of my life, unsure if I would survive or if I even wanted to, and all the while, I just needed to fully surrender to have complete healing! It may sound far-fetched, but truly, our healing comes from the surrender. In our darkest hour, He is there restoring our soul! He will lead us to a place of rest, but we have to trust His process and not question His steps.

Choosing to be happy, even when life gets you down, does not make you a bad person. On the contrary, it makes you strong and courageous! When you find yourself feeling guilty for even being here while finding your way to happiness, just dismiss it as an unsuccessful tactic of the enemy!

> Isaiah 41:10 (NKJV) says, "Fear not, for I am with you; Be not dismayed, for I am your God. I will strengthen you, Yes, I will help you, I will uphold you with my righteous hand."

Soon, I realized my fight was not with God. I was asking all the wrong questions about my progress. What could I learn from my grief? How could I help someone else overcome his or her heartaches? It was my choice to either be controlled by my grief or conquer it. I was praying for my season to end when, in fact, my blessing was in the *breaking*. Losing my brother and father were the end of fall catapulting me into winter. God never left me, He knew exactly where he needed me. So, He picked up the shattered pieces of my life and began to remake me so that He could use me. Like I said, I'm a warrior, so I chose the conquest to victory and it is a beautiful landscape.

*Chapter 4*

# SELF-DOUBT
## Insecurities and Comparison

"In order to be irreplaceable, one must always be different."
— Coco Chanel

Isaiah 43:4, NKJV: "Since you were precious in my sight, you have been honored, and I have loved you. . .."

S elf-doubt is the devil's way of distracting us from God's purpose. It's hard to be content in life when you want everything you don't have. Wanting that other girl's life leaves you feeling cast aside and less than. Don't get me wrong, it's okay to want more but not at the expense of hating yourself. Social media has launched us into an era where we see all the parts of another person's life . . . nothing is private! So, with online transparency, you have to be careful and not envy another girl's life. The time wasted scrolling through Facebook, Snapchat, or Pinterest could be setting you up for disappointment and creating a mind-set of "What I have is not enough." Trust me, the only portion of those other girls' houses that are "Pinterest Perfect" is the two-foot by two-foot shot that they posted today! I know this because I am guilty of it. I only post what I want my followers to see. I'm still human and have laundry, dishes, and toys everywhere.

Through my grief, I learned that if I wanted a better life than the one I was born into, it was up to me to create it. Was I capable and strong enough to do that? This was the question I constantly asked myself as I struggled through my newfound "lot" in life. There were so many things I didn't understand, but mostly, I wondered: *Why me?*

A struggle from rejection had already left me feeling that I wasn't good enough. I felt like a stray cat that no man would ever want . . . why would he?

My own father didn't want me. I thought I had to change and be something different, someone better. This was the start of a "dark path" journey that, still, as a thirty-two-year-old married woman, I fight.

I sat comparing my life with someone else's and soon found myself wishing I had an entirely different life. Living like this was pure and utter torture! This life we were designed to live is not even about perfection or worth! God's measuring stick is one without prejudice; His standard is far different from the standard of this world. His love has no comparison . . . it's not dependent upon our social status or breeding. Even so, it's easier to say this truth than to live it.

Self-doubt seems to take root the most when we see someone else living the life we dream of. But, it can also happen when someone else's *better* life is constantly thrown in our faces. You know when you are compared to someone by another person . . . have you been there?

<u>For example</u>: A mom always asking her daughter: "Why don't you make the 'A' honor roll like your cousin, or that girl at church? Why aren't you making plans to be in every club so you can look good to colleges? Why don't you learn an instrument like her? Why don't you clean the house like her? Why don't you get out and exercise the way she does?"

This daughter can only hear this so many times before she starts questioning her worth and value.

As a mom myself, I am careful not to compare my boys with anyone—or even each other. We see signs of "identity" loss when we are looking at someone else's life instead of our own. We are each unique and need individuality to live in true happiness. Seek to give compliments more than comparisons!

Find something you are good at and thrive at it, regardless of what everyone around you thinks you should be doing. Surround yourself with as much positivity as you can. No, you aren't perfect, but constantly feeling like a failure in everyone else's eyes will only derail your personal journey to self-love. Your success and how you view yourself shouldn't be contingent on anyone else. Let your bright personality shine no matter what. If you are insecure about who you are, change the people you are around.

*"Comparison is the thief of joy"* —*Theodore Roosevelt*

Joy is a feeling of great pleasure and happiness. It is something we are supposed to live in, every single day—not just a few days a year. When you become so focused on what everyone else wants you to be, you miss out on the moments where God desires for you to shine. Be who you were created to be and do it with complete confidence. Be totally unashamed of all your quirks, because guess what? We all have them!

I love day planners, pretty pens, and stationery. I don't "go with the flow" well, and spontaneous is certainly not in my vocabulary.

I like a well-thought-out and flawlessly executed plan. Heaven forbid if whiteout shows up in my beautifully color-coordinated calendar.

Make a plan, stick to the plan, properly execute the plan. I like stability, loyalty, and accountability. I don't like being thrown into an awkward or confrontational situation and I definitely don't enjoy being the topic of someone else's negative conversation. I don't like competition . . . if it should arise, most likely I will give up or bow out. Most of all, I like structure! Out of all these things, which seem rather simple to me, I see a trend. . .. I like to be in control of my life and, if I can help it, there will be no surprise outcomes. I also see that my need for approval from everyone around me can cause disappointment in myself. Based on what I've already told you about my childhood, you can probably understand why I love structure.

I hate to disappoint, mostly because I've spent so much time feeling like a disappointment and, as a child, assuming everything was my fault. I hate to be let down. I don't really know how to express what I want (and I don't like doing it, either) . . . which drives my husband crazy!

I started comparing myself to other girls at a very young age. I do understand that, sometimes, marriage doesn't last or work for any number of reasons. What I have a hard time wrapping my mind around is the leaving part. How can people walk away from a life, a person, a family that they vowed to be true to, without a care as to the turmoil left behind?

This lack of understanding about why, as a child, I wasn't "good enough" has turned into overthinking all my characteristics as an adult. I understand what it feels like to be unaccepted by a parent, to lose your sense of worth because he or she walked away and didn't look back. I just desired to feel wanted and like I had something to offer. Can you relate?

Fear not, friends, for I now know that happiness is attainable! You can have it if you are willing to put in the hard work. Comparison, measuring your life or possessions against others, does nothing for you but cloud your judgment. It forces you to see yourself through eyes of judgment and criticism. Learn to be completely happy just the way you are and be content with what you have and what you like. Simple things like style, food preference, favorite colors, brands, whether or not you like animals . . . those things are all negotiable and preferential, they are not heaven-or-hell spiritual matters, so just be you and be okay with it, even if your bestie doesn't prefer the same things you do.

We, as women—or even men—struggle with trial-and-error syndrome. After hours of scrolling on Instagram, we start clicking to buy that book, or those shoes that have changed someone else's life. I encourage you to take pause before you buy something. Ask yourself, is this me? If it's not, that's okay! *Something* else . . . whatever that is, will not make you happy or, better yet, fill the *ginormous* hole in your life or, more importantly, your heart. You can't keep cluttering your life with things that have empty meaning. Pretty soon you are going to wind up on one of those Netflix series, wondering how in the world you added so much chaos to your life.

What is your "something"? That thing that has you distracted from your purpose . . . what is it? Who is it? Maybe it's more than one thing, or maybe you have been on a journey of trial and error to figure it out. I have struggled many times with online shopping or taking interest in things, just because it seemed to be the thing that every other woman at my stage of life was doing, but did it truly make me happy? I have to be comfortable to be me! We spend far too much of our time trying to fit in and be accepted by making ourselves into something we are not.

My something is fear . . . more specifically, fear of rejection!

Whatever it is, that thing is stealing your joy and keeping you from your true potential so, find it . . . crush it . . . conquer it . . . change it . . . and move forward! Stop allowing every new and pretty thing to distract you from the BIG picture and that is: YOU! Dig deep! Do the work! Find where your hurts originate from.

I've been so afraid of being rejected again that I usually never tried. My insecurities run deep! There are more moments of doubt than confidence. I am so afraid of people not liking me because I'm not a certain size or style, that I literally overthink every single situation in my life. This is me—real-life, raw, and unfiltered Denisha talking to you right now. I was never smart enough! Fit enough! Pretty enough! There was always a better singer or musician than me.

If I am being really honest, I stopped writing this book at least a thousand times, for fear of rejection and relevance. It's so unhealthy when we forget how to love ourselves ... I mean *truly love ourselves*— despite "popular" opinion.

Fight for the girl you want to be! How much you want it will determine how hard you fight. Are you ready to be a warrior?

Here's the first thing you need to do: Love yourself!

When you can honestly say that you are happy with who you are, you can move on to the next step. Spend time reflecting on who you want to see in the mirror every day. What motivates you to be more? Where are your passions?

Next: Stop trying to be the girl across the room!

You know the kind of girl I'm talking about. That one on Instagram ... the one you've never even met in person? Don't you forget that her success is not your failure, so stop being so hard on yourself. I am a lover of pink ... all things pink. However, that doesn't mean you have to be!

Finally: Go and believe!

We take the easy way out when we place blame on everyone surrounding us. What I mean is, the conclusion of our stories are our decision ... we have the power to change the narrative. Believe you are worth it! *Changing your mind-set changes your outlook.* The power of believing is truly transformational!

Before you ask . . . let me tell you this:

1. <u>Yes, it is hard!</u> 2. <u>Yes, you can do it!</u> 3. <u>Yes, it is worth it!</u>

Through my childhood, teenage years, and even into early adulthood, I allowed so many things to determine my self-worth. I wrongly assumed that I needed to be the best dressed, most stylish, prettiest, most intelligent, and thinnest girl around in order to accomplish any of my goals.

That mind-set comes from having models and actresses in commercials, TV shows, magazine ads, and online. From a photo or a video, you are only shown their appearance—what they want you to see. What you aren't shown is that person's real life or true nature. Also, as I was a child of the 90s, the growing trend and goal was to be skinny!

Then came social media and the intensely competitive highlight reels. I was a new mom, thinking there was a serious problem. I mean, I must be sick because my house doesn't look like the highlight reels. So, clearly, I was failing at life, because there's no way on God's green earth my house was ever going to resemble those pictures. It's difficult to feel like we are getting ahead when we are staring at—and attempting to live—someone else's life. Someone's supposedly perfect life.

Girl, stop it! You are exactly who God wants you to be, now *own it!*

Stop questioning who you are or whether you can accomplish your goals, just because your life looks different from someone else's and she is doing what you feel will make you happy. Let me say it again: Stop it! You are your own precious design and God wants you to be happily content living the life He has created for you. No more negative talk and no more disdain toward yourself. I believe in you! I may not know you, but I truly believe in the power of change through positivity. I cannot stress the importance of loving yourself enough. Honestly, if we spent as much energy and time loving ourselves as much as we sought out the approval of others, our lives would be altogether different. By different, I mean joyful.

Do you know why? Because then we would be living in true, genuine contentment instead of being envious of a life that is not our own. We can't waste energy envying someone we've never even met. Life is not about what other people think about us.

If you are giving power to what others think of you, you are missing God's purpose in your life. That is not where fulfillment comes from—it comes from a close, personal relationship with God.

Your journey to overcome and defeat the presence of self-doubt in your life once and for all will be difficult. We live in a time where everyone's personal life is blasted all over social media every day. Everything can show up: the good, the bad, the private, the "oh my goodness, they should know better," even the stylish, and the selfie upon selfie. My point is: to each his own. Stop following people just to see their beautiful life that makes you sit, sulk, and dream that it was yours: that is torture! Maybe posting to stay relevant makes them happy, but it shouldn't make you feel like you aren't *enough*.

If you are allowing social media to dictate your worth and/or happiness, then take a break from it, reevaluate your purpose, and get back in balance. You will be happy you did and you will see just how much joy it has been stealing from your life.

> 2 Corinthians 10:12, NKJV: "For we dare not class ourselves or compare ourselves with those who commend themselves. But they measuring themselves by themselves and comparing themselves among themselves, are not wise."

Oh, my word, that scripture can preach to the women of 2019! It has become a favorite of mine and I pray that you, too, will see just how unwise and small-minded we become when we start playing this toxic comparison game!

I didn't always have the things the "important" girls in my youth group or school had, but my mom put her focus on what we did have and, I remember while their parents were too busy, my mom always had dinner with me and it was a meal that she prepared after a hard day at work. I remember the laughter we shared and talking about anything I wanted. Those moments meant more to me than designer clothes. It wasn't until I was an adult that I truly began questioning my worth, as I realized all the times that I needed my dad and he wasn't there. I had to learn in such a harsh way that I had a choice to make and only I could make it. I could either allow my mind to be ruled by self-imposed traps of comparison or I could completely surrender my thoughts and whole being to Jesus Christ, therefore living by His standard of grace and not the world's.

Choose to surrender, you deserve to be happy. The world wants to meet you, not the girl you are trying to imitate. Live free and whole, allow your mind to be transformed. Let yourself off the hook and be content in the grace that God desires to share with you. This comparison trend that is running rampant through generations of women is out of control and, in the process, we are passing the same insecurities down to the girls whom we are supposed to be raising strong!

There is a way to implement change and cultivate a new mind-set of confidence and happiness, but we will only experience it when we surrender to Christ.

I used to think confidence equaled self-centered, but that doesn't have to be true. We can express our individuality without cutting someone else down and validating her own doubts.

My father left me. He planted the first seed of self-doubt in my life and many more after that. His choices, early on, set me up for failure. It was a lonely and extremely insecure road . . . but for God's unending love! I'd lost hope and faith at a time when I needed it most. Growing up can be a cruel teacher, but we must remember we always have the power to change our story. You just have to stop feeling sorry for yourself long enough to stand up and say:

"No more! Today, and from this day forward, I will fight!"

Rejection will not have the final say. I will prevail with God on my side and I will live a life full of love and acceptance. Just like God knows my ending, He knows yours! Trust Him even when you can't see where you are going. He knew I would be okay and find my way out of the hard times, as long as I kept my faith in Him strong. He was preparing a young man's heart and molding his personality to perfectly fit with mine. All I had to do was be patient.

> Proverbs 3:5–6, NKJV: "Trust in the Lord with all your heart, and lean not on your own understanding; In all your ways acknowledge Him, and he shall direct your paths."

We must be careful to not allow comparisons to cloud our vision, launching us on a thousand voyages that will never lead us to our true desire. Take intentional time in prayer and seek God's will for your life.

While you wait on Him, be patient and know that He will work all things for your good. Why? Because He values you and all that you bring to the Kingdom. He created you in His image. Trust that His majestic design is far better than anything you could ever create for your life. That day at the cemetery, when I prayed for God to show me how to access His fountain overflowing with healing, He spoke to me, just as the sun peeked out of the clouds. I felt His warmth flood my spirit and I clearly understood that by completely surrendering to His will, I would never thirst again. As long as I stay plugged into Him, I will be full of life, I will come alive, and my brokenness will have served a purpose. Be confident in who He says you are! The images of waterfalls flowing from the cross have never been clearer to me! My self-doubt has no place in my divine purpose in Christ and neither does yours.

*Chapter 5*

# Fountain of Grace
## Waves of Healing

"New beginnings are often disguised as painful endings."
— Lao Tzu

Zephaniah 3:17, NKJV: "The Lord your God in your midst, The Mighty One, will save; He will rejoice over you with gladness; He will quiet you with His Love, He will rejoice over you with singing."

My well was empty and dry until I opened my heart to Jesus and allowed His will to take root in my life. The moment I lowered barriers that only I had built, God filled me with His overflowing fountain of grace. We can't operate from an empty well! I know I talk about my mom singing a lot, but again, I am going to reference a song that she used to sing and that I sang at my brother's funeral:

*"Peace, peace, wonderful peace coming down from the Father above.*
*Sweep over my spirit forever I pray.*
*In fathomless billows of love."*

I prayed so fervently for that precious peace to cover my life and overwhelm me. Something that is "fathomless" cannot be measured or understood. Quite similar to saying, "peace that passes all understanding," we were never meant to fully understand all the awesome acts of God. His grace, peace, and mercy are some of those unexplainable things. Peace gives the impression of being very deep, mysterious, and complicated. All we have to do is trust God and He will drop that sweet sensation into our spirit.

I wanted to do more than survive, I wanted to thrive . . . I wanted to feel guiltless happiness. Our identity doesn't have to rest upon our trials of grief; we can grow through them and cultivate the life God desires us to have.

What I didn't realize in the beginning of my journey from grief to grace was that I had easy access to my freedom. My key to healing was found in Jesus. See, the moment I received the Holy Ghost and accepted His spirit in my heart, I gained possession of the most significant gift to utilize my healing. What a beautiful and accessible provision He has given me. I am now and forevermore a child of God! A royal princess. Our breakdown comes when we allow our grief to captain our progress instead of God's grace.

Hebrews 4:16, NKJV: "Let us therefore come boldly unto the throne of grace, that we may obtain mercy, and find grace to help in time of need."

I could have started this book with this very scripture and left every other page blank. It says it all. When you are grieving in your spirit, there is only one thing to do! Go! Get up and go boldly before His throne of GRACE in your time of need! There is an old familiar place that we can go for healing and restoration! God is waiting on us to run to Him. He died on a cross for you and for me, and there is a beautiful wave of mercy that flows from that cross. It's like a waterfall, and who doesn't like a beautiful waterfall! Everything we need to thrive is there; He is ready to pour it on your life! I thank God that I found that majestic waterfall of grace and mercy, which allowed healing into my life. I love to sing, so, as a singer I would just begin singing praises to His name and in that melody, a beautiful overflow of grace began to happen. I had to be willing to relinquish my title as a victim in order to hold my shield of victory.

Once the hard work of overcoming rejection was complete, I could move forward with my healing. I truly believe the scars remain as reminders of our journey. It's not always about the finished product. Sometimes, or dare I say most times, it's about the process. Even when it stings!

Did you know we can have physical responses to emotional problems?

I recently started seeing a holistic doctor for my out-of-control hormones. I learned that my body was reacting to emotional damage that stemmed from my childhood. It's absolutely bizarre how our bodies were created. I sat on this table talking (possibly too much) to this perfect stranger. One question led to another, then another. She listened to me self-diagnose and overshare for more than an hour.

Finally, she said, "Your problems started long ago."

Umm . . . duh! I could have told you that. As she stood there and continued blowing my mind with truths about my life that I didn't even tell her. I cried and hung my head.

But she said, "Don't be ashamed, I want to help you find healing."

God sure does know whom we need in our path. I told her that I firmly believed in spiritual healing, but along the way, I was harming my body by holding all my hurt inside. This doctor prayed with me and helped me see the damaging effects of stress. I am still walking my road to healing and I sometimes slip and fall, but when that happens, I take a moment to sit and drink from His glorious fountain of grace.

We can always count on God's grace and His love. In our loneliest of moments, He's right there holding out His arms to offer you comfort.

We can't blame Him, or even the devil, for every bad thing that's ever come our way. Most of the time, it's just life and, unfortunately as a child, the bad choices that your parents make will affect you more than anyone else. My husband knows better than anyone that trust never came easy to me. I worked so hard, but that was after I made him beg for me to not make him pay for my father's mistakes. I am so ashamed that I ever made him feel like he didn't deserve my trust. . . .. I was damaged goods and yet, he loved me.

Closure, or lack of it, caused so much of the emotional top-sy-turvy in my life! My father rejected me, which I struggle with because it was his choice— I don't need a therapist to tell me why I have issues with self-worth. However, not having the chance to ask him: "Why?" Well, that to me is the heavier baggage—like paying Delta an unexpected $300 more at check-in kind of baggage. That's a lump-in-your-throat, kick-you-in-the-stomach, knife-in-the-heart kind of hurt!

I still sometimes find myself searching for approval. Am I good enough? Will they like my hair? Are my shoes stylish? Am I funny? Do I talk too much? Am I pretty enough? This is when I remind myself that God has made me in His image and I will shine. It's not about the approval of others, remember? I have to keep my heart purposed in Him and shield myself from doubt. Rejection changes the way we think about ourselves! It puts a false reality into our innermost thoughts and that is when we begin all the negative self-talk.

Be encouraged! There *is freedom in healing*. However, that will only happen when we take a step-by-step approach, focusing on forgiveness! We typically throw ourselves into anything and everything instead of just dealing with our inside hurts. I mean, truly addressing the problem! We have to take the time to be completely honest with ourselves. Doing that will save so much confusion and wasted moments.

Every mile of heartache, every lonely weekend, every cold visit to a jail phone, every time I enthusiastically answered a collect call only to hear, "Let me talk to your brother." Every look of disapproval validated my biggest fear of being less than all the other girls, who lived in functional homes.

Those moments led me to the arms of a man wise far beyond his years. They molded me to be his wife. He is far more than I deserve and everything I prayed for, and then some. When he walked into my life, I was damaged and tattered, then I became broken and still, he loved me! I would say God was in the middle of that. Never postpone a chance for joy if life brings it along.

I have learned that the broken pieces of my heart remain broken, but I have managed to seal the cracks, and with God, I have redesigned the empty places. Broken can be fixed, if you want it badly enough. Do you want it badly enough? God's power has been at work in me from the very beginning, even when I didn't feel it, see it, or know it. He was waiting on me. We live moments, good or bad, for a purpose.

Enduring is the key: we must be willing to endure the process. There is beauty in the unfolding, but if we can't get out of our own way and relinquish our grip to God's grace, then we will forever be stuck. We will relive an excruciating cycle day after day until we surrender. Simply and unapologetically surrender; it won't be pretty, but as you shed every bad memory, you will become more and more of the person God has called you to be. He doesn't want us to keep our agonizing moments on *repeat* and punish ourselves day after day with grief.

Stand boldly and surrender your trials to God. Stand sacrificing all your pain and grief to Him. He will repurpose your energy to a greater, more fulfilled life. His love is unfailing!

*Chapter 6*

# THY WILL BE DONE
Finding God's Will in the Midst of My Pain

Matthew 6:10, NKJV: "Your Kingdom come, Your
will be done, on earth as it is in heaven."

T here is nothing quite as painful as being in a crowded room
yet feeling alone! Loneliness has stolen many moments from
me . . . moments that should have been joyful. Meanwhile, there was
a Savior standing with arms wide open, waiting on me to become
ready for a moment of demolition. I needed to ready my spirit and
flesh for my own personal "Demo Day"! When we tear down the
walls that we have been so crafty to construct, we are essentially
saying: "<u>Thy will be done!</u>"

As I mentioned in chapter 1, I often heard my mom singing the
old song "He's Been Faithful," and now as an adult, I apply the words
to my everyday life. Through the many trials, I've learned fear of
rejection will keep me from my destiny in Christ. I cannot live a life
of fear and doubt if I want to grow and move forward. Though we

can't live in fear, there are moments of fear and we must remember that we serve a God who will wipe every one of them away.

When we find ourselves in the middle of a trial or just life, what do we do? How do we endure the process? It's very simple, we trust!

Ephesians 3:14–21, NKJV:

14. "For this reason I bow my knees to the Father of our Lord Jesus Christ,

15. from whom the whole family in heaven and earth is named,

16. that He would grant you, according to the riches of His glory, to be strengthened with might through His spirit in the inner man,

17. that Christ may dwell in your hearts through faith; that you, being rooted and grounded in love,

18. may be able to comprehend with all the saints what is the width and length and depth and height.

19. to know the love of Christ which passes knowledge; that you may be filled with all fullness of God.

20. Now to Him who is able to do exceedingly abundantly above all that we ask or think, according to the power that works in us,

21. to Him be glory in the Church by Christ Jesus to all generations, forever and ever. Amen."

Hard as it may be, after experiencing a life full of rejection and self-doubt, a life with disappointment and broken promises; we choose to trust Him. In order to fully see His will unfold in our life, we must be willing to tell our flesh "No!" To learn not to be a "Debbie Downer," although it is way harder than it sounds and again I will say, it takes hard work and sacrifice to be completely in God's will. How badly do you want it? How badly do you want to experience happiness? You can't thrive off drama and want positive change! Those two do not work hand in hand. I know you are probably laughing right now and yelling, "Are you kidding me? Seriously?" Don't throw the book across the room just yet. This is not meant to discourage you! It's just like anything else in life, whether it be fitness, lifestyle, diet, or career, or whatever area of your life you need victory in.

Nothing good and successful comes without hard work. All this sounds good and, if you're anything like me, you have a highlighter in hand right now gearing up for a mind-blowing quote! Just remember, when the sting of rejection pricks your heart, don't give up! *Don't give up!* Please, don't give up. Life is full of ups and downs, it's surrounded by disappointments and loss but just don't quit! Like Christopher Robin says: "You are braver that you believe, stronger than you seem, and smarter than you think."

Even though you feel powerless, press forward! Full steam ahead! Believe me, I know how much effort it takes. Yes, I understand how scary it can be and life most definitely will be unpredictable. Even so, allow God to be your guide and find your power in Him. When we have Him, we have all fullness and all the strength we need to conquer our circumstances!

> Hebrews 13:6, NKJV: "… The Lord is my helper, I
> will not fear. What can man do to me?"

I am so thankful that we can count on God's love every time! No matter what life throws at you, no matter the amount of times people let you down, He is always there. For most of my life, my focus was on my brother. Detention, suspension, boot camp, community service, court hearings, juvenile, police officers, probation officers, and rehab facilities all played a part in his life and my mother's and my lives, too. I saw my mom's pain, even when she tried to be strong for me. I saw the aching heart of a woman just trying to find happiness. Her agony was all the motivation I needed, to know that I didn't want the life my dad crafted, the life my brother followed him into. Mostly, I didn't want to disappoint her and make her life any harder. I wanted laughter and sunshine! I didn't want the affliction that accompanied drugs and alcohol!

My constant prayer was that I would allow my pain to shape me into God's image. That I could stand in awe of the awesome work He'd accomplished in my life. I want to be able to say that when things went bad, then became much worse than I could have ever imagined, I stood firm and heard that still, small whisper that I was His. God knows your every care. His love is unfailing and I was experiencing this firsthand. My spirit was heavy and I was heartbroken, but He was near and I could feel Him. However, I had to believe, and I mean truly believe, that I was worth His love.

We have to be willing to accept the *breaking process* in order for Him to whisper a graceful blessing into our moment of need. Our faith can shift the atmosphere of any situation, so it doesn't really matter what storm you're sitting in the middle of, as long as you have faith you can shift your focus and remove fear immediately. That is when grace is activated in your life.

God's grace is such a beautiful gift; it's something that can't be bought or even earned. It's free and we only need to open our hearts to receive it. I am so thankful for that gift in my heart. I am grateful to be a child of such a caring, heavenly Father. I am blessed to know His grace and that, no matter where we are in life, that grace is present. It doesn't matter where you stand in life, His grace is right beside you and all you have to do is open your spirit to welcome it in.

> Luke 1:37–38, NKJV: "For with God nothing will be impossible. Then Mary said, Behold the maidservant of the Lord! Let it be to me according to your word. And the angel departed from her."

Mary's story has always been one of my favorites. She no doubt overcame gossip and persecution, then mothered a child, whose fate she knew would be devastating. Even so, she stood and endured the agony of losing Him. She was brave enough in this scripture to say, "Be it unto me . . ." Accepting a higher calling, knowing that understanding God's will as it unfolded in her life wouldn't be easy, she still humbly accepted her fate. Her attitude was: "Whatever it takes, God, I am your servant and I am willing to do the hard work."

This verse pushes me to be a better Christian, a better woman, a better servant, a better person. I want to be strong enough at the end of the day to say, "God, I humbly accept Your will in my life. I understand there will be heartaches and possibly stumbling blocks along the way, but I want to serve You, in spite of my hard times, and sing hallelujah from my darkest valley. Thy will be done, God, in my life as it is in heaven. Amen."

*Chapter 7*

# ROAD TO RECOVERY
### Finding Grace Right Where I Am

After years spent grieving and ignoring my problems, I went back to the cemetery and said my final goodbye. Everything was out in the open and I purposed in my heart to not just acknowledge my issues but put in the hard work to fix them. I promised myself that day that, no matter what, my life would not end unhappily. I remember watching the sun peek out from the clouds and I knew then that I was in control of my story. The sunshine was God's subtle nudge at my heart, encouraging me to trust Him. Oh, how foreign trust was to me, but I was willing to try. Anything was better than the clouds of sorrow the enemy was leading me to.

I could make the choice to fight my family tree and what was expected of me or I could concede and become another branch taken over by sin. The choice to live—loved and in God's will—was mine alone. I could change my path. I could have more, and God wanted me to come to Him for healing. I had a choice to walk a righteous, imperfect path of restoration with God, or I could choose anguish and torment with the enemy.

It didn't take long for me to realize I wanted the sunshine. Everything is perfect in God's timing. You see, three months prior to losing my brother, I walked fearlessly into a relationship with the man I now call "husband." I knew so quickly that I would spend forever with him! Had I not been surrounded by his crazy love for the church and God, maybe I wouldn't have been brave enough to take a leap in faith. I completely immersed myself in my local church.

The nagging pain was still there and I spent some days choking on my grief, but I pushed and fought my way forward. I knew I was holding on to a promise, and if I would wait and be patient on the potter's wheel as it was molding me, soon I could find peace in my storm. The molding and "being worked over" hurt, but the end product would be a beautiful design, crafted by Jesus.

Can I tell you a secret? You can make it! You are enough!

Take your journey one day at a time and when you stumble, don't give up! Take a breath and redirect! It's not about how fast you finish, it's about getting to the finish line. When you feel hopeless, look inside and remember you are a warrior! Be brave and have courage.

> 2 Timothy 1:7, NKJV: "For God has not given us a spirit of fear, but of power and of love and of a sound mind."

We have no reason to fear when we have God on our side. If you reach deep, I mean really dig to the depths of your soul, you will find there is strength and your key to activating that strength is: *you get up and fight*. At first, you may feel numb and possibly empty, but the more you work, the more you see that you can do it! Too often we allow negative voices to validate our insecurities of not being enough. Stop that right now. That is not at all what God desires for your life, He wants to see you smile more and enjoy the beautiful opportunities that are anxiously awaiting you.

Remember, day by day, step by step, you will conquer!

> Isaiah 54:17, NKJV: "No weapon formed against you shall prosper, And every tongue which rises against you in judgment you shall condemn. This is the heritage of the servants of the Lord, And their righteousness is from me, says the Lord."

> Psalms 46:10, NKJV: "Be still, and know that I am God; I will be exalted among the nations, I will be exalted in all the earth!"

Sometimes when we just stand still, the grace of God finds us. That has to be the hardest part of our journey, being still. Giving complete control means we are no longer calling the shots, instead we are trusting God to be our guide, the Captain of our ship! I love the water. It's where I feel perfect peace and the grandeur of God's design. The waves bow to the storm, yet they are flexible enough to regain composure and carry on preparing for the next surge.

**So, here's my question: How badly do you want it?**

How badly do you want your life to change?

Have you hit rock bottom? Trust me, you will know if you haven't already and when you do, hopefully it's not comfortable. You can't improve your circumstances if you aren't willing to work hard: it's not a magic pill you can take, where you wake up to a grand life full of glitter and sparkle.

When we constantly complain about our circumstances and we are crying out for help, yet we shoot down every solution offered ... you don't want it badly enough.

It's just like wanting to advance in ministry: we only want it if it requires zero sacrifice and minimal change on our part. Sometimes our problems don't require a solution, we just need a dose of maturity to outgrow them.

I once heard someone say, "People want progress without change."

The issue with that is, they go hand in hand. Progress can't happen without change. It might be uncomfortable and have an out-of-your-box mentality, but if you want more, you have to change. Are you truly ready for the life you deserve? You know, the beautiful life that God has designed for you? He's waiting for you to welcome Him in so that He can mold you like a piece of clay. It sometimes hurts as you wait on Him to completely fulfill His will in your life but be patient and don't give up. He wants you to experience happiness and joy.

*"Into every garden a little rain must fall."*
*—Ella Fitzgerald*

My garden should be luscious and full of every flower under the sun. I know that without my trials and without my grief, I would have never become such a vivid picture of grace. My story was crafted through many years of mixed emotions, false promises, and disappointments. There were several long-lost dreams, but through my process, I found purpose and focus. I have vowed not just to myself, but to my brother and father's memory to take this testimony of God's grace and share it everywhere I can. The storms of life come raging; they wreak havoc any and everywhere, affecting all walks of life. We can't let our circumstances be our downfall!

I want my story to say: I defeated everything that was meant to destroy me. I want to always remember that God's love never fails and His mercy is new every morning.

You were meant for more: stop believing the lie that you aren't enough!

I know that holding on to a past full of hurt and rejection will not benefit me; in fact it will harm or stunt my spiritual, emotional, and physical growth in every way. Bitterness, resentment, and anger are deep-seated emotions that turn into terminal diseases! Forgiveness is our freeing cure.

So, yes, you guessed it correctly—I chose the road of forgiveness. I forgave my father for everything he did to me. I let go of all the rejection and started seeking God's acceptance, instead of acceptance from everyone around me. I forgave my brother for leaving me.

I finally gave myself permission to grieve and learned that it didn't make me weak, as long as I didn't give it a permanent residence.

I learned that I didn't need answers to have closure. You know, even if my dad could have provided me with an explanation of his choices, it wouldn't have been sufficient. I needed him and he wasn't there. That is a fact, but thank goodness I found a Father who could be all that I needed and more.

> Esther 4:14, NKJV: "Perhaps this is the moment
> for which you have been created..."

Sometimes in our grieving moments all we have to hold on to is a promise that we wish will be fulfilled. A promise that will bring hope instead of heartache as we wonder, will this be another broken word or will it actually work in my favor? In those moments when you are holding on, find confidence in the fact that you are known. You as a person have value and your worth is far greater than you realize.

Those moments of darkness can define you, they can shape you and the choice is yours. Will you be crushed or will you conquer? When life gets hard and you feel like everything is spiraling out of control, you may be walking numb, in a constant state of wonderment. *Do you hear me, God? Am I worth fighting for? The world around me has forsaken me, but you, God, are you there?*

Yes, the answer is yes! He hears you and you are not alone!

Your story may look different than mine. Grief doesn't always equal loss. You can grieve over any number of situations. When you find yourself surrounded by darkness and sitting alone curled up in a corner, remember you are known. I want to encourage someone in this moment—boy, girl, man, woman—I want to encourage you today. You do have value!

You are so much more than you think you are! You are known by a gracious Father! You are not obsolete! If you can reach down deep and grasp the fact that you have a heavenly Father who is here and holds you in such high esteem, you will make it.

The knowledge of God's grace is enough to get you through whatever trial you are facing at this moment. It could be a trial of the heart, it could be a trial of the mind, or like me, it could be a trial of circumstances beyond your control that someone else masterminded. No matter what the trial is, you hold to the fact that you are known and friend, you will make it through!

All you need is the courage to believe in yourself, because He already does and so do I! If I can face all the challenges life has thrown and continues to throw at me, so can you. Believe you are more, know you are enough and suit up, my friend!

Bringing my story to a close, I realize that without the grief, without the trials, without the hurt that became the puzzle pieces of my life, I wouldn't be living the life I am. I wouldn't be a pastor's wife today. I wouldn't be Michael's wife! I wouldn't be Corban and Logan's mom. I have learned through so many different disappointments and heartaches that those things, those trials that we go through, those tears that we cry . . . they shape us and they make us into the men and women of God whom we are destined to be. I may not have received the blessings that I have received in my life had I not gone through the hurt and the pain. I may not have the friends I have today had I not walked the roads that I have walked. I most certainly wouldn't have a voice of influence in the lives of students and young adults. I am confident that every single choice that I made in my life brought me to where I am today.

As a young adult, I learned that you can't please everyone. I was struggling to just feel accepted and defined as my own person instead of being prematurely judged based on my father's choices or my brother's decisions. I wanted to be Denisha and just Denisha!

That seventeen-year-old girl was literally drowning in someone else's mistakes; I was being punished for the sins of my household and prevented from moving forward in Christ—all because people saw the worst in me! I am thankful to know a God who sees the best in me. Can you say amen?

I made a choice to walk away from the life I was living in 2003 and that choice was the best and possibly the scariest decision of my life. I left the only church I had ever known, one where I became a lonely bitter girl. I was raised in a small Pentecostal church where I stood out as the daughter of a homeless drug dealer. I made a choice to redefine who I was and to recreate my reality. I didn't even know that was possible but, step by step, I began believing in myself. Having said that, that decision cost me a great deal. It cost me family, it cost me friends, and it cost me mentors. But, in the end, it was well worth it! I saw who truly had my back and my eyes were opened to what it truly meant to be a Christian. See, I thought I knew what it meant to be a godly person but really, I had no clue. Being a Christian is about showing the world God's love. It's about opening our hearts to love people that aren't kind. We, as Christians aren't called to judge and hurt each other. You will find in life that when you make unpopular decisions, however hard they may be, if God is in the middle of them—you cannot fail! I was just a kid, struggling to find my place in the world. Little did I know when I decided to change my life and do what was right for me, I was just days away from walking into the lowest, darkest valley of my life. I was about to be shaken to my core and feel lonelier than I ever had before. God knew what He was doing and He knew exactly where I needed to be to endure the grief that was ahead of me. There was one person though, one constant in the transitional time, one who told me that if I would keep my focus on Jesus Christ, I would make it always.

That person was my mother. She told me that she would support my decision to make this change in my life as long as I could promise her that I wouldn't walk away from God. I kept my promise; I found a church that loved big and accepted me for who I was. Soon, I noticed growth happening in my spirit. This is where I found my husband.

And this is where my healing began. This is where I now serve as the pastor's wife, can you believe it? A stringy-haired, rejected, cast aside, stopped-believing Christians-were-actually-Christians kind of girl now gets to call herself a pastor's wife. It can happen to you, too! Don't let anyone tell you that you are going to be worthless because you come from brokenness! Don't you dare accept the lie that you have unworthy DNA coursing through your body! You can be anything you want to be regardless of where you come from. I am proof that it is possible.

I recently learned that your *gifting* is different from your *calling*. My entire life, I was gifted and talented in music and I assumed that God wanted me serving in that capacity. I began praying and seeking Him because, after five years leading a music program, I was still broken, lost, and hungry for more. One Sunday, I was really crying out to God and a minister came to me and said, "Write the book." So, here I am, two years later, finishing what God has called me to do—write. At the same time, we had a young man move to Georgia and take over our music department. I'm telling you, God never fails us and He always honors your sacrifice. I spend my time writing and speaking now; it's what God has called me to do. All the moments of grief up to this point have shaped me into who I am today. It's not about me and what I am doing, but what God has done through me and how He has made all my imperfections *work*.

He has blessed me beyond measure and turned all my grieving moments into a graceful masterpiece.

I never had to go out in search of grace, it was here all along. God's grace has been present in every phase of grief and I always knew just how to find it. God is always working on me and for that I'm thankful. Be patient and learn to show yourself grace, because if I've learned anything, it's that healing doesn't happen overnight. It's a process and small progress is great progress.

When God strips us of all the things that make us feel safe and secure, He gives us a story far better than we could have written for ourselves. Grace is, after all, an exercise of love and kindness. God shows each of us a measure of grace and we, too, must extend that to each other. You and I truly can't go wrong walking in grace, love, and kindness.

1 Corinthians 13:8, NKJV: "Love never fails. . .."

Grace wins.

CPSIA information can be obtained
at www.ICGtesting.com
Printed in the USA
FSHW021400040619
58698FS